If You Were the MOON

Laura Purdie Salas   illustrated by Jaime Kim

Millbrook Press/Minneapolis

Helloooooooooo up there, MOON! I'm sooooooo tired.

I wish I could do exactly nothing, just like you.

But I do so many things, child.
And if you were me, you would too.

If YOU were the MOON,
you would . . .

Hover near your mother.

Scientists believe the moon formed 4.5 billion years ago when a meteorite the size of Mars collided with the newly formed Earth. Rock from Earth and the meteorite splashed into space, and the moon was born.

Help keep her in balance.

The Earth wobbles as it spins. The moon's gravity, the force that pulls other things closer, reaches out like an invisible pair of hands to steady the Earth. Without the moon, Earth's wobble would be wilder! Extreme swings from scorching heat to frigid cold would destroy most life on our planet.

Spin like a twilight ballerina.

The moon spins on its invisible axis, making a full turn every twenty-seven days. It also circles around the Earth once every twenty-seven days. Because it spins on its axis at the same speed that it circles the Earth, we always face the same part of the moon. We call the side that never faces Earth the dark side of the moon.

Play dodgeball with space rocks.

The moon would not be good at dodgeball, because it doesn't get out of the way of the meteorites crashing into it! All those collisions have pounded the top layer of the moon's crust into gray, powdery dust. Craters and dents pit its rocky surface.

Hide in the shadows.

The moon goes through different phases as it orbits the Earth each month. When the moon is between the Earth and the sun, we can't see it because the sun's light is hitting the part of the moon that we are not facing. We call this a new moon.

Tease the Earth:
peek-a-boo!

The moon appears to wax (emerge from darkness and grow to a full moon) and wane (shrink from full moon back into darkness) every 29.5 days. The moon does not really grow and shrink! We just see different amounts of the moon, depending on the location of the sun, moon, and Earth.

Catch and throw. Catch and throw.

At night, the moon seems to glow in the sky. But the moon is made of rock. Like the Earth, it does not create any light. Instead, the moon "catches" light from the sun and "throws" it toward Earth.

Challenge the ocean to a tug-of-war.

The moon's gravity pulls on the Earth. As that gravity tugs at our oceans, it creates high tides and low tides. Meanwhile, the Earth's gravity also pulls on the moon. The moon has no oceans or tides, but scientists believe the Earth's gravity pulling on the moon has caused thousands of small cracks and ridges in the moon's surface.

Be a bright alarm clock to wake the night.

As daylight fades, the night world awakens. Nocturnal animals rest during the day and hunt, feed, mate, and communicate at night. Owls and ocelots and hyenas and hamsters are just a few of our night world's nocturnal creatures.

Light a pathway to the sea.

When sea turtle eggs hatch onshore, the hatchlings instinctively scurry toward the brightest light. That is usually moonlight sparkling on the ocean, calling the tiny turtles to their home in the sea.

Weave a spell over wonderers.

The moon inspires artists all over the world. French composer Claude Debussy wrote "Clair de Lune" for piano. American poet Emily Dickinson wrote "The Moon Is Distant from the Sea—." The Baule people of the Ivory Coast craft wooden moon masks for festivals.

Wait for friends to visit again.

Besides Earth, the moon is the only body in space earthlings have walked on. Twelve astronauts walked on the moon between 1969 and 1972—Neil Armstrong was the very first. Because the moon has no wind, their footprints will stay imprinted in the dusty surface for a million years or more.

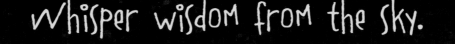

Whisper wisdom from the sky.

For centuries, the moon has guided farmers. American growers used to plant, weed, and harvest crops during certain moon phases. In China, people still celebrate the fall harvest and eat moon cakes on the fifteenth day (a full moon) of the eighth lunar month.

Sing Earth a silver lullaby.

For my sister, Janet,
guiding light for wandering creatures —L.P.S.

For Jaeho —J.K.

Glossary

axis: an imaginary straight line through the center of the moon

gravity: the force that draws one object to another. Earth's gravity keeps us from floating away.

meterorite: rock or metal that lands on the surface of a body in space

orbit: to travel around something else in a curved path

phase: the shape of the part of the moon we can see at different times

tide: upward and downward movement of the level of the ocean

Further Reading

Chin, Jason. *Gravity*. New York: Neal Porter Books, 2014.

Lin, Grace. *Thanking the Moon: Celebrating the Mid-Autumn Moon Festival*. New York: Alfred A. Knopf, 2010.

Marino, Gianna. *Night Animals*. New York: Viking, 2015.

Pendergast, George. *The Phases of the Moon*. New York: Gareth Stevens, 2016.

Shepherd, Jodie. *To the Moon!* Minneapolis: Millbrook Press, 2017.

Singer, Marilyn. *A Full Moon Is Rising: Poems*. New York: Lee & Low Books, 2011.

Yolen, Jane. *Owl Moon*. New York: Philomel Books, 1987.

Acknowledgment: Thank you to astrophysicist Shelbi R. Schimpf for reviewing the text and layout for accuracy.

Text copyright © 2017 by Laura Purdie Salas
Illustrations copyright © 2017 by Jaime Kim

Millbrook Press
A division of Lerner Publishing Group, Inc.
241 First Avenue North
Minneapolis, MN 55401 USA

For reading levels and more information, look up this title at www.lernerbooks.com.

Designed by Danielle Carnito.
Main body text set in Coffeedance 32/18. Typeface provided by Chank.
The illustrations in this book were created using acrylic paint and digital techniques.

Library of Congress Cataloging-in-Publication Data

Names: Salas, Laura Purdie, author. | Kim, Jaime, illustrator.
Title: If you were the moon / Laura Purdie Salas ; illustrated by Jaime Kim.
Description: Minneapolis : Millbrook Press, [2017] | Audience: Ages 5–8. | Audience: K to grade 3. | Includes bibliographical references.
Identifiers: LCCN 2016019757 (print) | LCCN 2016024990 (ebook) | ISBN 9781467780094 (lb : alk. paper) | ISBN 9781512428384 (eb pdf)
Subjects: LCSH: Moon—Juvenile literature.
Classification: LCC QB582 .S25 2017 (print) | LCC QB582 (ebook) | DDC 523.3—dc23

LC record available at https://lccn.loc.gov/2016019757

Manufactured in the United States of America
5-50313-18721-3/5/2021